D1210041

Mark R. Levin:
The Liberty Amendments
Restoring the American Republic

By Quick Read Summary Books

Table Of Contents

INTRODUCTION

The attempt to undermine the United States Constitution has been ongoing for almost a decade. It is now necessary to restore constitutional principles of a republican government. Such efforts are usually heavily opposed by those wishing to retain an aristocracy. The fourth section of the fourth article of the constitution states "the United States shall guaranty to every state in the Union a republican form of government." There are no other conditions; this directive is absolute. The republican government, one that is representative of the people's will, founded on the principle of individuals elected by citizens, is to be guaranteed, and is the very form of government the United States set out to preserve.

The current government is rapidly turning into an authoritarian government, one that threatens civil liberties, and the very type of government the first settlers risked everything to escape from. This transformation is marked by "a centralized and consolidated government with a ubiquitous [present or found everywhere] network of laws and rules actively suppressing individual initiative, self-interest, and success in the name of greater good and on behalf of a larger community."

These principles that embody an authoritarian government are called Progressivism, and may sound logical on the surface, but are fraught with oppression.

The nation has entered what is described as "post constitutional soft tyranny," in which the original intent of the U.S. Constitution has slowly eroded over time into a state in which the citizens are easily manipulated and controlled. President Obama has vandalized the constitution by making new laws, ignoring existing ones, and exploiting the very language of the law to serve his own self-interests. This phenomena is possible because the federal government itself has slowly evolved into a governing body that oppresses and ignores, not serves, the will of the American people.

Most members of the current House and Senate have been wooed by Obama's self-proclaimed genius, hunger for power, and feigned godliness, subscribing to his agenda in the name of the "greater good." New policies, touted as reform and improvement measures, are imposed, even though they have no established basis on which to justify them by any rational means. Alexis de Tocqueville, the French thinker and philosopher who came to America in the early 1800's, explained the development and characteristics of such a government with much foresight, "It covers the surface of society with a network of small complicated rules, minute and uniform, through which the most original minds and the most energetic characters cannot penetrate, to rise above the crowd.

The will of man is not shattered, but softened, bent, and guided; men are seldom forced by it to act, but they are constantly constrained from acting. Such a power does not destroy, but it prevents existence; it does not tyrannize, but it compresses, enervates, extinguishes, and stupefies a people, till each nation is reduced to nothing better than a flock of timid and industrious animals, of which the government is the shepherd."

Reforms introduced by the government are written in language that sounds pleasing, but veils the details that reveal their true purpose-- control. By delegating power to unauthorized administrators that comprise a de facto fourth branch of government, the Administrative State, laws are imposed that escape accountability, for the Administrative State's power is derived from spanning all three traditional branches of government.

The manner in which policy changes are imposed on the very people they represent is designed to weaken the individual and empower the governing bodies. Regulations and rules are ambiguous and convoluted, difficult if not impossible to comprehend, and overwhelming to the average person, who sees no choice but to simply comply.

In response to Congress' failure to meet his demands and pass laws that he wants, President Obama has repeatedly told Congress "if [it] won't act soon to protect the future generations, I will!" He has ruthlessly done just that, by allowing executive branch agencies and divisions to assume the role of all-in-one law maker, interpreter and enforcer, circumventing the American people altogether. While Obama defines this as "compassionate progressivism," history defines it as despotism, an authoritarian or dictatorship that is often cruel and oppressive.

Just as Congress has failed to check the executive branch in its claim of absolute power, the judicial branch has similarly failed to protect the Constitution. The judicial branch was explained by Alexander Hamilton as "…the least dangerous to the political rights of the Constitution; because it will be lease in a capacity to annoy or injure them." This branch's purpose, which is clearly described by Alexander Hamilton in Federalist 78, is to faithfully ensure that the separation of powers and the Constitution is protected free from politics and pressures from outside parties, particularly large corporations and the other branches of government. It has, however, claimed the role of the final decision-maker on all matters, from which there is no remedy.

Even the Supreme Court makes mistakes, for they are all human, and the three most notorious blunders in history are Dred Scott v. Sanford, endorsing slavery; Plessy v. Ferguson, affirming segregation; and Korematsu v. United States, upholding the internment of Americans.

The Court has effectively taken it upon itself to rewrite parts of the Constitution including the Commerce Clause and the tax provisions, to justify the federal government's interference in private economic activity. In addition, the Court has interjected its own personal preferences in social, cultural and religious issues, most of which should have been handled by lower courts.

What was to be a limited government, and certainly not harmful, has morphed into a force that has little to no accountability, serving as the nation's largest "creditor, debtor, lender, employer, consumer, contractor, grantor, property owner, tenant, insurer, health-care provider, and pension guarantor." What it does not command, it overregulates, micromanages, or simply prohibits. There are no limits to the ways the federal government uses harassment and fear-tactics to manipulate society to accomplish its goals. The Framer's unequivocal intent was to preserve the States as primary governing bodies, and the federal government as a supportive structure to maintain a cohesive union, nothing more, with the majority of governing power residing at the state level.

Finances do not create an obstacle, either, for when the federal government uses what it seizes from its citizens, it turns to endless borrowing, driving the national debt to unmanageable amounts. This leads to "quantitative easing" by purchasing its own debt, issuing itself credit, and printing more money.

The federal government consumes a quarter of goods and services produced each year in America, and under this administration has accumulated an operating deficit of over $17 trillion, as opposed to the historical average deficit $1 trillion. The annual wealth created each year by U.S. citizens doesn't come close to covering what is spent.

The American people must put their federal government back in line, or conditions will continue to spiral out of control and private bank accounts will dwindle as more personal finances flow out of the hands of the rightful owner and into the hands of a government that will continue to spend recklessly.

The consequences of these practices, although the federal government has turned a blind eye and deaf ear to them, are inevitable. The currency devalues, significant inflation or deflation occurs, and the economy itself becomes shaky.

This leads to the logical next step of raising taxes, "There is also serious talk from the governing elite about instituting a national value-added tax (VAT) on top of existing federal taxes…and divesting (depriving) citizens of their 401 (k) private pension plans" in addition to the state and local taxes citizens already must pay. The bigger picture, however, is gloomier. The nations of Cyprus, Spain and Greece already illustrated the outcome of fiscal irresponsibility, and America is well on its way to being in the same boat.

The solution is again found in Tocqueville's observations, "it is new in history of society to see a great people [citizens] turn a calm and scrutinizing eye upon itself when apprised by the legislature that the wheels of its government are stopped, to see it carefully examine the extent of the evil, and patiently wait two whole years until a remedy is discovered, to which it voluntarily submitted without it costing a tear or drop of blood from mankind." Our system of government was designed for the citizens of this nation to determine that an elected official's representation is unsatisfactory, and to vote him out of office in the next election. It is imperative for the American people to now examine the unsustainable condition of our government and the Founding Fathers' intentions, as well as the foundation set forth by the Declaration of Independence, and the Constitution itself.

The Administrative State and the Framer's Constitution cannot coexist. It is the American citizens' responsibility to learn history, understand the Framer's intentions, and to diligently assess the current state of government, insisting on the return to a government "...of the people, for the people, by the people..."

Complacency is not an option, and the government is too far out of control for it to correct itself. The majority of our nation's leaders are so wrapped up in their own narrow-sighted, greedy, immoral and hazardous behavior that they are incapable of appreciating the foundation on which this country was established. The American people must take responsibility for their governance, rescue themselves, and re-establish balance before it is too late. America must be returned to the great nation she was once.

To do so requires four fundamental steps: one, American citizens must acknowledge that their federal government is no longer faithful to the Constitution; two, the people of America must understand the urgency of the current condition, and to fully realize that action is required to prevent the ultimate death of their free country; three, the American people must be enlightened, clear in their understanding of the course to take to restore balance the way it was originally intended; and four, the American people must find and use the courage necessary "to confront—intellectually and politically—the Statists' hunger for power. "

8

The Framers designed the federal government to be intentionally limited in power. As a matter of fact, the Constitution would not have been ratified without this being a primary consideration. The priority was safeguarding state sovereignty. There were two schools of thought at the time: the Federalists, who believed in a central government as the primary governing body, and the anti-Federalists, who believed states should be the primary governing bodies. History documents the many debates in which the Federalists repeatedly reassured the anti-Federalists that the federal government would be limited. In Federalist 45, James Madison insisted "The powers delegated by the proposed Constitution to the federal government are few and defined. Those which are to remain in the State governments are numerous and indefinite."

The powers vested in the central, or federal, government, were only those essential to preserving the Union. Madison was not alone in his declarations; rather, he was the voice of the commonly-held beliefs of the Framers of the Constitution; therefore, the final draft that was ratified diversified authority and affirmed a system of checks and balances, clearly declaring that states maintained the decisive role in governing the nation. After all, the states established the federal government.

Article V of the Constitution provides two options for proposing amendments to the Constitution, intentionally preventing Congress from being the only entry-way for proposing an amendment, for, as Mason described, a Congress who has already become oppressive would never agree to the consideration of an amendment proposal that would limit its actions.

The process for proposing an amendment, therefore, reads "The Congress, whenever two thirds of both houses shall deem it necessary, shall propose amendments to this Constitution, or, on the application of the legislatures of two thirds of the several states, shall call a convention for proposing amendments, which, in either case, shall be valid to all intents and purposes, as part of this Constitution, when ratified by the legislatures of three fourths of the several states, or by conventions in three fourths thereof, as the one or the other mode of ratification may be proposed by the Congress..." The first option has resulted has resulted in 27 amendments, while the second option has never been used.

Article V also affords state legislatures notable authority to restore our founding principles should the federal government overstep its bounds, forsake its original purpose, or simply grow too powerful, as was the Founding Fathers' concern. The possibility was at the center of discussions during the original Constitutional Convention, and the possibility of less-than-honorable men at the highest levels of government succumbing to selfish pursuits, intoxicated by their own power, was high because of the laws of human nature. As a result, the Framers saw fit to be proactive rather than leave the Constitution vulnerable, and were diligent in clarifying that nothing in this process was left to Congress' discretion.

Today's reality dictates tremendous difficulty in amending the Constitution, for many efforts have fallen short. Remember, only 27 amendments were ratified out of the over 1000 amendments that were attempted. The current government will make it even more difficult, for they no doubt will resort to desperate tactics, using their media partners and their assumed power to suppress the American public, making every effort to block endeavors to once again return balance to the federal government. Evasion has been their hallmark, and the unfamiliarity of not only government officials, but also American citizens, of the intricacies of the Constitution would serve their interests.

The contemporary American public often resigns itself to the notion that a grim future is inevitable, accepting defeat without lifting a finger to stop it. This book is written for those very citizens, to provide a lawful and civilized manner in which to repair the damage before it is too late.

The American public has tremendous power to reign in an out-of-control government and to "reestablish self-government and secure individual sovereignty." The American public must fully realize their freedom to do so.

AN AMENDMENT TO ESTABLISH TERM LIMITS FOR MEMBERS OF CONGRESS

On the surface, there is nothing wrong with continually returning elected representatives to Congress if the people think that they are doing an adequate job representing their constituents; however, the reality is that the longer the representatives' tenure in Congress, the longer such officials push for gerrymandered political districts to make reelection easier, become insulated from the people they represent, entrenched in an artificial reality that has led to their losing touch with the realities about American society, and are more focused on reelection than serving.

Further, the longer a Congressman remains in office, the easier it is to woo and influence constituents and other supporters, such as large corporations, all using federal funds. Our Congress today is largely characterized by these self-serving interests, all at the expense of lost liberties and property of the individual. Ronald Rotunda, a Chapman University law, admits that "office rotation in the British House of Lords and the former Soviet Politburo has a higher rotation than that of the United States Congress." In 2010, 85 percent of the incumbents in each house were reelected. Stepping back, in 2008, the year that Barack Obama was first elected, 94 percent in the House and 83 percent in the Senate retained their seats in Congress.

During the 18th century, many of the colonies such as Pennsylvania, Virginia, Delaware, New York, Massachusetts, and South Carolina all had some sort of provision that required office rotation such as flat out term limits, or not being able to serve consecutive terms in their respective legislatures. In fact, the United States' first governing document, The Articles of Confederation included a provision that stated "no person shall be capable of being a delegate for more than three years in any term of six years..." During the ratification debates of the new federal Constitution, although not present during the Constitutional Convention, Thomas Jefferson wrote a letter to James Madison on the principles of office rotation stating: "I dislike, and strongly dislike ... the abandonment, in every instance, of the principle of rotation in office, and most particularly in the case of the President..."

The concept was clearly not one of professional or lifetime public service, but of service on a part-time and temporary basis, including strong participation by the citizens of the nation, necessary to curb governmental abuse of power. Members of Congress were, in fact, encouraged and even expected to maintain their careers in the private sector. In addition, the rather short terms for the members of the House as well the president were intended to ensure steady rotation of office-holders, and this is clear throughout study of the writing of the Constitution. Benjamin Franklin issued a riveting warning about human behavior, stating "...there are two passions which have a powerful influence on the affairs of men.

These are ambition and avarice; the love of power and the love of money...The struggles for them are the true sources of all of those factions which are perpetually dividing the Nation, distracting its Councils, hurrying sometimes into fruitless and mischievous wars, and often compelling a submission to dishonorable terms of peace. And of what kind are the men that will strive for this profitable pre-eminence...It will not be the wise and moderate; the lovers of peace and good order, the men fittest for the trust. It will be the bold and the violent, the men of strong passions and indefatigable activity in their selfish pursuits...The more the people are discontented with the oppression of taxes; the greater the need the prince has of money to distribute among his partisans and pay for the troops that are to suppress all resistance, and enable him to plunder at pleasure." Franklin, as well as the rest of the Framers, attempted to make holding office in the federal government unappealing to people who hold those traits, not only by expecting terms to be limited, but also by limiting financial compensation. Wages for government officials were modest at most until the middle of the twentieth century. In spite of their cautious nature, the Framers gave humanity too much credit for being honorable and able to regulate its innate selfish desires. Professor Mark P. Petracca of the University of California explains, "The oft-touted expertise of professional politicians as representatives stands in stark contradiction to the essential function of political representatives who share their values and stay in touch

12

with the reality of their day-to-day lives."

Turnover in Congress averaged 50 percent with each election until President Franklin Roosevelt ran for and won a third term in 1940, as well as a fourth in 1944, in the midst of World War II. This led to the Twenty-Second Amendment which limits the president to two terms, or, in the case of a vice president taking office because of a president's death or other cause of his no longer in the office, finishing the predecessor's term if it is half over as well as two full terms. World War II, however, provided special circumstances upon which the Progressives quickly capitalized.

They used the war to substantially increase their own power, marking the first time in American history that the government became intrusive and significantly more dominant. Movement into the heart of economic, social and cultural aspects of our country was swift, adopting the Sixteenth Amendment to collect income taxes and repealing the Seventeenth Amendment and state representation in the Senate, as well as ignoring the Ninth and Tenth Amendments, designed specifically to limit such movements by the federal government.

The proposed amendment is not a new concept; on the contrary, the limited terms for presidents is still viewed favorable, and most states today have term limits for state-level offices. The American people have lost faith in Congress, consistently providing low approval ratings that keep getting lower. Approval of Congress' performance and ability to faithfully represent the will of the people was rated 19 percent in 2010, 17 percent in 2011, and 14 percent for the first half of 2013. Term limits and more frequent rotations would significantly shift this very revealing data.

AN AMENDMENT TO ESTABLISH TERM LIMITS FOR SUPREME COURT JUSTICES AND SUPER-MAJORITY LEGISLATIVE OVERRIDE

The Framers were prophetic in their anticipation of potential problems and abuses. They were concerned about a president becoming a tyrant, so they created a powerful legislature and an independent judiciary to mitigate this possibility. They were also particularly conscientious in providing measures that prevented one branch of government from becoming so powerful that it consumed the others. One of these measures is Congress' authority to determine the number of justices on the Supreme Court and the configuration of the federal court system under it. In most instances, Congress also determines the various jurisdictions of the federal courts, both original and appellate, and may impeach and remove most federal officials, including the president under certain circumstances.

The judiciary had to be free from "undue influence," but still needed strings to keep it closely fitting in a republican government. The judiciary's purpose was to interpret the legal and constitutional applications in federal civil and criminal cases brought before it, with no involvement beyond that narrow definition. It was not given authority to judge federal laws at their own discretion, nor may they legislate, or make laws, including reviewing bills under review in the legislature.

The Framers' intentions to create limitations on the ability of any one branch or level of government to have unanswered authority over the other is infinitely clear; however, as with the legislative and executive branches of government, the contemporary Supreme Court has moved beyond the scope of constitutional boundaries and willingly involves itself in legislating in virtually every aspect of the lives of the American people. No longer is the judicial branch of government as Alexander Hamilton described in Federalist 78, "Whoever attentively considers the different departments of power must perceive, that, in a government in which they are separated from each other, the judiciary, from the nature of its functions, will always be the least dangerous to the political rights of the Constitution; because it will be least in a capacity to annoy or of the strength or of the wealth of the society; and can take no active resolution whatever." Hamilton continued, "It may truly be said to have neither FORCE nor WILL, but merely judgment; and must ultimately depend upon the aid of the executive arm even for the efficacy of its judgments.

This simple view of the matter suggests several important consequences. It proves incontestably, that the judiciary is beyond comparison the weakest of the three departments of power; that it can never attack with success either of the other two; and that all possible care is requisite to enable it to defend itself against their attacks. It equally proves, that though individual oppression may now and then proceed from the courts of justice, the general liberty of the people can never be endangered from that quarter; I mean so long as the judiciary remains truly distinct from both the legislature and the Executive."

No longer is the judiciary the "least dangerous" branch of the federal government, having become just as intrusive and dangerous as the other two, and "there can be no doubt that were the conditions that exist today—with the Supreme Court involving itself in minute and endless facets of everyday life—known to the convention delegates, they would undoubtedly endorse a check on judicial authority."

In Anti-Federalist 11, Brutus, who was believed to be New York judge and Anti-Federalist Robert Yates, as well as one of the most articulate opponents of the Constitution, was alarmed. He warned that "The real effect of this system of government, will therefore be brought home to the feelings of the people, through the medium of the judicial power. It is, moreover, of great importance, to examine with care the nature and extent of the judicial power, because those who are to be vested with it, are to be placed in a situation altogether unprecedented in a free country. They are to be rendered totally independent, both of the people and the legislature. No errors they may commit can be corrected by any power above them, if any such power there be, nor can they be removed from office for making ever so many erroneous adjudications."

The 1803 Supreme Court decision in Marbury v. Madison would have horrified Yates. Chief Justice John Marshall's decision asserted, "The judicial power of the United States is extended to all cases arising under the constitution. Could it be the intention of those who gave this power, to say that, in using it, the constitution should not be looked into? That a case arising under the constitution should be decided without examining the instrument under which it arises? This is too extravagant to be maintained." The Supreme Court used this case to claim authority that the Framers did not grant in the Constitution, and, as predicted, abuses have followed.

The Marbury decision caused Thomas Jefferson grave concern, as it was completely contrary to the Constitution that only grew with age. In 1820, he wrote William Jarvis, "[T]o consider judges as the ultimate arbiters of all constitutional questions [is] a very dangerous doctrine indeed, and one which would place us under the despotism of an oligarchy. Our judges are as honest as other men and not more so. They have with others the same passions for party, for power, and the privilege of their corps . . . and their power the more dangerous as they are in office for life and not responsible, as the other functionaries are, to the elective control. The Constitution has erected no such single tribunal, knowing that to whatever hands confided, with the corruptions of time and party, its members would become despots. It has more wisely made all the departments co-equal and co-sovereign within themselves."

Several decades later, President Abraham Lincoln had to contend with the Supreme Court's 1856 decision in the notorious Dred Scott v. Sandford case, in which the Court determined that Scott, a slave, could not sue for his freedom because he was not a citizen, for only the white race could be citizens. This case also declared that Congress did not have the authority to ban slavery in the states. During his first inauguration speech in 1861, Lincoln said, "I do not forget the position assumed by some that constitutional questions are to be decided by the Supreme Court, nor do I deny that such decisions must be binding in any case upon the parties to a suit as to the object of that suit, while they are also entitled to very high respect and consideration in all parallel cases by all other departments of the Government. And while it is obviously possible that such decision may be erroneous in any given case, still the evil effect following it, being limited to that particular case, with the chance that it may be overruled and never become a precedent for other cases, can better be borne than could the evils of a different practice.

At the same time, the candid citizen must confess that if the policy of the Government upon vital questions affecting the whole people is to be irrevocably fixed by decisions of the Supreme Court, the instant they are made in ordinary litigation between parties in personal actions the people will have ceased to be their own rulers, having to that extent practically resigned their Government into the hands of that eminent tribunal. Nor is there in this view any assault upon the court or the judges. It is a duty from which they may not shrink to decide cases properly brought before them, and it is no fault of theirs if others seek to turn their decisions to political purposes."

Less than half a century later, Woodrow Wilson, a leader of the Progressive movement and the twenty-eighth president, serving from 1913 to 1921, did just that, starting a destructive ball rolling that has led to an extreme shift from the original Constitution in which "The Court has so fundamentally altered its duties, and so completely rejected the limits placed on it by the Constitution's checks and balances and enumeration of powers, that the justices are in an endless search for extra-constitutional justifications and interventions to explain their activism."

Whatever one may think of the Marbury decision, it cannot be denied that today the Supreme Court's has continued to roll the ball in the direction that Wilson started. The Court has handed down numerous politically decisive judgments, nearly all of which expand federal power, including its own, directly and knowingly contradicting the Constitution's structure and limits. On such occasions, the justices "contort the facts and the law, as they must, to reach their desired result." In the 1942 Wickard v. Filburn case, the Court ruled erroneously that the federal government has authority to regulate limitless forms of private economic activity, including the production of goods and services for one's own use or use within a state.

In the 1947 Everson v. Board of Education decision, it voided the long-standing balance between government and religion, demolishing the "wall of separation" between church and state, that lead to the overt detriment of religious freedoms in the country by banning of prayer, nativity scenes, and crosses, "among other forms of religious expression," in public places across the United States.

In addition to the Dred Scott decision, the Court's capacity for grievously trampling the foundational principles of this country found in the Constitution is glaringly apparent in the 1896 Plessy v. Ferguson holding, where the Court endorsed racial segregation in public facilities under the doctrine of separate but equal and in the 1944 Korematsu v. United States decision, where the Court gave authority to the U.S. Army to confine tens of thousands of Japanese Americans without due process, and Roe v. Wade, the 1973 ruling in which the Court legalized abortions, again with no constitutional basis.

Judicial review can be exercised for good and bad; it can be exercised wisely and foolishly. The Court has a well-documented history of both; however, the nature of its rulings over the past century have fundamentally overstepped its bounds with giant steps. By adding the proposed override, for the first time justices will no longer be solely judged by history, but by the people who ultimately must live with their decisions, as it should have been all along.

As James Madison once wrote, "As the courts are generally the last in making the decision, it results to them, by refusing or not refusing to execute a law, to stamp it with its final character. This makes the Judiciary department paramount in fact to the Legislature, which was never intended, and can never be proper." The proposed amendment seeks to address what, in fact, has come to pass.

TWO AMENDMENTS TO LIMIT FEDERAL SPENDING AND TAXING

Congress and the President have refused to adopt a budget for the past four years, resulting in sequestration. Obama assumed that the mandatory across-the-board eight percent budget cuts, as a result of sequestering, would force Congress to adopt the budget he wanted—it did not. Meanwhile, both attempt to hide political responsibility from the public while continuing to increase spending. This is not a matter of simply electing the right people; rather, it is a matter of removing the overwhelming political incentive to recklessly spend.

Both the executive and the legislative branches of government are in open violation of the Congressional and Impoundment Control Act of 1974, requiring Congress to submit a budget resolution, laying out its planned financial disbursements, as well as a timetable for completing its final budget for the president to sign or veto. Since 2010, Congress has passed 17 different continuing resolutions to avoid complying with the Budget Act's requirements, passing numerous interim spending bills as well as several ridiculously voluminous omnibus bills that are not even comprehendible.

 A prominent member of Congress recently describe it as "So voluminous was this monster bill that it was hauled into the chamber in an oversized box. Its thousands of pages, which the clerk hadn't even time to number, had to be tied together with a rope, like newspapers bundled for recycling. While reading it was obviously out of the question, it's true that I was permitted to walk around the box and gaze upon it from several angles, and even touch it."

The Budget Control Act of 2011 was adopted to enforce the Congressional and Impoundment Control Act of 1974, and it states: "For the purpose of enforcing the Congressional Budget Act of 1974 through April 15, 2012 ... the allocations, aggregates, and levels set in subsection (b) (1) shall apply in the Senate in the same manner as for a concurrent resolution on the budget for fiscal year 2012." The

Budget Control Act is more substantial than the usual budget resolution. First, it is legally enforceable, unlike a budget resolution that never even goes to the President. Second, it sets discretionary caps for 10 years, instead of the customary one year. Third, it is enforceable, including a mechanism for two years of "deeming resolutions," which allow specific aspects of the budget to be enforced. And fourth, it creates a "Super Committee" process to address both entitlements and tax reform. It backs that process up with a $1.2 trillion sequester. Obama and Congress have broken a system that was already straining, "their opportunism and dysfunction threaten a financial implosion that presages the eventual collapse of the nation's currency and economy, resulting in unimaginable devastation and misery." Therefore, a constitutional amendment is the only way to impose restraint.

The norm for this administration is to raise the debt limit, a total of eleven times so far, increase federal fiscal spending, which in has risen $1.79 trillion since 2002, and to operate on a massive federal deficit, landing at $1.32 trillion in 2012. Increases in the federal deficit mean increases in overall federal debt.

The increase in the federal debt based only on fiscal operations was 104.8 percent of the gross domestic product (GDP) in 2012. By 2022, the reasonable projection for the federal debt resulting solely from fiscal operating expenses exceeds $25 trillion. None of this includes the total unfunded liability of major entitlement programs, such as Medicare, which is expected to consume 10.4 percent of the GDP by 2086. The total accumulated debt resulting from fiscal operations plus all unfunded liabilities is over $90 trillion.

As if that weren't enough, for the first time in America's history, the nation's credit rating has been downgraded by Standard and Poor, the credit rating agency, from a perfect AAA to AA+ with Standard and Poor's note that our country's outlook for the future was grim. American's credit rating can be downgraded again in 2014 should the rating agency see a less than desirable decrease in spending, higher interest rates, or new fiscal pressures during the rating period.

The federal government has also been warned by the Government Accountability Office (GAO), who report that it is on a path to destruction, insisting on practices that cannot be sustained. Continuing on the current path, the country will face eventual economic collapse.

In response to all of this, the Federal Reserve has add to the calamity by granting itself the power to influence the country's credit and financial settings to pursue full employment and a stable economy. This includes full regulation of banks and stock markets, as well as inserting itself into the nation's payment system, manipulating interest rates, printing money, forcing private banks to buy federal debt, create an endless line of credit with nothing to back it, and devaluing the dollar. Seven members of the Federal Reserve Board and five of the twelve Federal Reserve Bank presidents granted themselves unregulated power and formed the Federal Open Market Committee to carry out these monumental tasks.

The need to limit the federal government's spending habits corresponds directly with the need to restore the Constitutional limits on levying taxes, and this was a central concern in the state ratification conventions for adopting the new Constitution.

In Democracy in America, Alexis de Tocqueville warned that unending meddling by the federal government was a risk for the country based on the very nature of democracy, "In democratic societies…there exists an urge to do something even when the goal is not precise, as sort of permanent fever that turns to innovation of every kind. And innovations are always costly." Amos Singletary, father to nine children and a grist mill operator, was more direct in a speech during the Massachusetts Ratification Convention, in which he declared, "We contended with Great Britain—some said for a tree-penny duty on tea, but it was not that—it was because they claimed a right to tax us and bind us in all cases whatever. And does this Constitution not do the same…they tell us Congress won't lay dry taxes upon us, but collect all the money they want by impost. I say there has always been a difficulty about impost…they will not be able to raise money enough by impost and then they will lay it on the land, and take all we have got.

These lawyers and men of learning, and monied men, that talk so finely and gloss over matters so smoothly, to make us poor illiterate people swallow down the pill…they expect to be managers of the Constitution themselves; and get all the power and all the money into their own hands, and then they will swallow up all us little folks like the great Leviathan, Mr. President, yes, just as the whale swallowed up Jonah."

The Massachusetts delegation did vote for ratification, but urged an amendment that would provide that monies raised from impost and excise taxes were not sufficient for justifiable national purpose, Congress could requisition a state. Only if a state did not pay or refused to pay the requisitioned amount could Congress levy a tax on the state directly. No change was made, however, because the consensus was that the limited power set forth in the Constitution was obvious. Congress was to provide the funds for only three purposes: to pay debts, to provide a "common defense," and to provide for "the general welfare of the United States." Supreme Court associate justice Joseph Story reiterated this in the 1830's by saying "A power to lay taxes for the common good and general welfare of the United States is not in common sense a general power [a power to lay taxes for any reason]. It is limited to those objects. It cannot not constitutionally transcend them."

The Framers clearly did not grant Congress the general power to tax. Several attempts in the late 1800's to enact a general income tax were subsequently struck down as unconstitutional. The federal government was finally successful in 1909 when President William Taft urged the passage of the 16th amendment and it was passed quickly by Congress that same year. Three-fourths of the states ratified it by 1913, compelled by the argument that it shifted the burden of taxation to a broader base. The resulting income tax was initially modest at best, but Progressive nurturing over the years has sent income taxes collected by the federal government through the roof, fueling increased federal spending as well as federal thirst for more. The rhetoric that the federal income tax was protecting people The federal income tax process has become so cumbersome for the American people that US taxpayers spent nearly 61 billion hours to prepare filings in 2012, with 60 percent of taxpayers hiring someone to do it for them, and another 30 percent using online tax preparation software.

The federal government's self-appointed power to tax has overtaken private areas of American people's lives as well. The Affordable Care Act, also known as Obamacare, distorts the government's right to tax further and damages a sector of private commerce, the healthcare industry, compelling an individual to purchase services and products, regardless of ability, mandated by the federal government. The administration completely "ignored legislative history, the actual text of the statute, the Court's precedent, and the Constitution's text to redefine Obamacare's penalty provision as a tax." In addition, the IRS is granted authority to enforce the key provisions of the law, which precipitated the hiring of thousands of additional staffers and the creation of committees, offices and teams to implement it.

The proposed Tax Amendment will cap the income tax rate at 15 percent, and eliminates all forms of double taxation, such as the death tax. It also moves the tax filing deadline from April 15 to the first Monday in November, shortly before Election Day, to prevent the realities of the taxpayers' lives from disconnecting from the candidates and accountability. It will also disband the current IRS bureaucracy and simplify the system, removing an undue burden from taxpayers shoulder.

The proposed Spending Amendment would force Congress to address the spending and budgeting catastrophes, and would work with the Tax Amendments to reform unfunded major programs. Both Amendments would pull the federal government back within the limits originally intended by the Framers, staving off the tidal wave of destruction looming over us.

AN AMENDMENT TO LIMIT FEDERAL BUREAUCRACY

When we were children, we learned about the three branches of government and that the Constitution granted and limited the powers for each of them. Separation of powers was clear, as were specific roles of each branch, as well as the system of checks and balances. Checks and balances, however, were never meant for any branch of government to act outside its jurisdiction.

As James Madison wrote in Federalist 48, "It is agreed on all sides, that powers properly belonging to one of the departments ought not to be directly and completely administered by either of the other departments. I do not conceive that power is given to the President and senate to dismember the empire, or to alienate any great, essential right. The exercise of the power must be consistent with the object of the delegation." John Locke, the most widely read philosopher during the American Revolution, echoed this in his Second Treatise of Government. He added that the legislature "in not the only supreme power of the commonwealth, but sacred and unalterable in the hands where the community have one placed it…There are bounds which we trust, that is put in them by the society, and the law of God and nature, have set to the legislative power of every common-wealth, in all forms of government."

It is apparent that the separation of powers doctrine was of infinite importance to the Framers, and, as with the other provisions of the Constitution, was never meant to be redefined or ignored altogether. They believed that they had agreed upon a document that would allow the government to govern, and to retrain themselves from stepping outside the carefully crafted boundaries set forth. The Supreme Court upheld the Framers' intention in 1892, when the decision issued in Field v. Clark made it clear that for Congress to delegate lawmaking authority to the executive branch would breach the Constitutional provisions.

Franklin Roosevelt introduced the New Deal in the 1930's and

1940's, allowing Congress to pass laws creating new agencies and delegating power for these agencies to have unlimited regulation of the economy and daily life. The Supreme Court initially struck down these laws, but Roosevelt threatened to replace members with those of his choosing to accomplish his goals. While the Supreme Court changed its course and began upholding his efforts, Roosevelt eventually did replace sitting justices with me who shared his ideas about government.

One of his closest advisors, James Landis, professor of law at Harvard, voiced justification for Roosevelt's dismantling of many foundational principles of the Constitution by saying, "…the administrative process springs from the inadequacy of a simple tripartite form of government to deal with modern problems." This line of thought was used to create a vast federal bureaucracy, destroying representative government and mangling separation of powers.

The expansion of the federal bureaucracy brought a plethora of regulations that cost $236 billion in 2012 to monitor compliance. Currently, the Federal Register, the publication that documents all administrative rules, exceeds 77,000 pages. In addition, the number of criminal offenses that an individual can be guilty of in any given day, offenses that these regulations created, are so numerous that nobody has been able to count them. The current state of affairs "makes congressional oversight, political accountability, and rational reform mostly impracticable if not impossible."

The administrative state's practice of creating agencies and regulations outside the scope of documented legislative practices is in abundance and almost completely unchecked. The Supreme Court, usually eager to exercise their powers of judicial review, has avoided matters dealing with administrative agencies by deferring to members of Congress, who created them and certainly isn't going to limit or disband them.

To make matters worse, presidents are quick to use the administrative state's process to circumvent Congress whenever members do not enact legislation that the executive branch wants.

All of this is in complete opposition to the official process for authorizing new regulations, which includes allowing for public comment and actually considering public comment when determining whether the proposed regulatory provisions should be granted or denied by Congress. Contrary to the process, comments are primarily sought from groups who have a stake in the outcome, and comments solicited from the public are done so as a mere formality.

Private parties wishing to challenge a final rule must file a costly lawsuit within 60 days of the formal announcement of the new regulation. Filing a petition with the U.S. Court of Appeals for the District of Columbia Circuit is not only costly, but time-consuming, potentially taking years for a single matter to be resolved. The Supreme Court also rejected the Constitutional separation-of-powers doctrine, declaring it nonviable. In addition, the Court presumes that the regulation in question is valid and reasonable unless proven otherwise, putting all of the burden of proof on the petitioner. The rule will be upheld if the agency can provide a rational basis for it. "Rationally based" has yet to be defined, and therefore has endless possibilities for manipulation.

The proposed amendment to reduce the federal bureaucracy is designed to discontinue the collusion of the three branches of government in dismantling the Constitution. By returning to the states the Constitutional provision of regulating private economic activity, we reduce the burden of the federal government's oppressive control on private citizens. In addition, the proposed amendment would require Congress to justify the existence of current agencies within three years of adopting the amendments, and would undo the unconstitutional rewriting of the Constitution that has steadily gained momentum over the years.

AN AMENDMENT TO PROMOTE FREE ENTERPRISE

The Commerce Clause of the Constitution declares that Congress shall have the power "[t]o regulate Commerce with foreign Nations, and among the several States, and with the Indian Tribes." In 1996, the Late constitutional scholar and Harvard law professor Raoul Berger elaborated in 1996 that the "focus on trade alone was not fortuitous; the Framers were fastidious in their choice of words. For them, 'trade' did not, for example, include agricultural production, which plainly was 'local.' In the Convention, George Mason said that the 'general government could not know how to make laws for every part [state]—such as respects agriculture.' And [Alexander] Hamilton wrote in Federalist No. 17 that 'the supervision of agriculture and of other concerns of a similar nature . . . which are proper to be provided for by local legislation, can never be desirable cares of a general jurisdiction.' In Federalist No. 12, he adverted to the 'rivalship that once subsisted' between agriculture and commerce. . . . Hamilton referred separately in Federalist No. 36 to 'agriculture, commerce, [and] manufactures' as 'different... kinds' of 'wealth, property, and industry,' not as fused in commerce. In sum, the Founders conceived of 'commerce' as 'trade,' the interchange of goods by one State with another... Madison stated that it was necessary to remove 'existing & injurious retaliations among the States,' that 'the best guard... was the right in the Genl. Government to regulate trade between State and State."

 Given the jealous attachment to state sovereignty, the absence of objection that the Commerce Clause invaded State autonomy indicates that such an intrusion was simply unimaginable. [Thomas] Jefferson accurately reflected the Founders' views when he stated in 1791 that 'the power given to Congress by the Constitution does not extend to the internal regulation of the commerce of a state . . . which remains exclusively with its own legislature; but to its external commerce only, that is to say, its commerce with another state, or with foreign nations... 'That no more was intended was made clear by Madison in a letter to J. C. Cabell: 'among the several

States'…grew out of the abuses of the power by the importing States in taxing the non-importing, and was intended as a negative and preventive provision against injustice among the States themselves, rather than as a power to be used for the positive purposes of the General Government…"

In 2001, Randy E. Barnett, Commerce Clause expert and Georgetown University law professor, carefully scrutinized the original meaning of the Constitution's Commerce Clause. After carefully studying the Constitutional Convention and the Federalist Papers, as well as the state ratification debates, Barnett "found…that the term 'commerce' was consistently used in the narrow sense and that there is no surviving example of it being used in either source in any broader sense."

The Federalist Papers also used this same narrow definition of "commerce," and to further explain, Barnett wrote, "In Madison's notes for the Constitutional Convention, the term 'commerce' appears thirty-four times in the speeches of the delegates. Eight of these are unambiguous references to commerce with foreign nations which can only consist of trade. In every other instance, the terms 'trade' or 'exchange' could be substituted for the term 'commerce' with the apparent meaning of the statement preserved. In no instance is the term 'commerce' clearly used to refer to 'any gainful activity' or anything broader than trade…In none of the sixty-three appearances of the term 'commerce' in the Federalist Papers is it ever used to unambiguously refer to any activity beyond trade or exchange…Having examined every use of the term 'commerce' that appears in the reports of the state ratification conventions, I found that the term was uniformly used to refer to trade or exchange, rather than all gainful activity."

Barnett concluded with "…if anyone in the Constitutional Convention or the state ratification conventions used the term 'commerce' to refer to something more comprehensive than 'trade' or 'exchange,' they either failed to make explicit that meaning or their comments were not recorded for posterity."

The late constitutional scholar Robert H. Bork, as well as attorney

Daniel E. Troy, examined the Constitution's Commerce Clause as well, and they concurred with Barnett's conclusions, stating "Early American writings distinguish 'commerce' from the class of subjects to which it is separate but connected in two ways: either by a direct discussion of what is excluded from commerce, or by implication. Alexander Hamilton's writings in the Federalist Papers provide many of these definitions by implication. Hamilton often included 'commerce' in a list of concepts which are similar in one way (activities critical to the success of the nation, for instance), but distinct enough to call for separate identification, as in 'the state of commerce, of arts, of industry.'

These early discussions of the nature of the Union suggest that 'commerce' does not include manufacturing, agriculture, labor, or industry. In short, 'commerce' does not seem to have been used during the founding era to refer to those acts that precede the act of trade. Interstate commerce seems to refer to interstate trade—that is, commerce is "intercourse for the purposes of trade in any and all its forms, including the transportation, purchase, sale, and exchange of commodities between the…citizens of different States."

Some find it difficult to imagine America surviving under this code of commerce, yet this was American enterprise at its earliest days. The Framers' intentions were clear, and are to this day. Commerce did not refer to agriculture or manufacturing, indicating that the Framers did not intend the federal government to govern without significant and effective limits. "The separation of the three concepts, in other words, indicates a significant and purposeful limitation to the commerce."

Associate Justice Joseph Story wrote rather extensively in the 1800's about the Constitution, and his commentary is considered some of the most notable regarding this subject. Story wrote in the language typical during the time the Constitution was drafted and ratified. Commerce, manufacturing, and agriculture were clearly separate and distinct areas of economic activity, and noted in the Federalist Papers that "'commerce' was not a catchall to describe all three." Story observed "It is hardly possible to exaggerate the oppressed and degraded state of domestic commerce, manufactures, and agriculture, at the time of the adoption of the Constitution. Our ships were almost driven from the ocean; our work-shops were nearly deserted; our mechanics were in a starving condition; and our agriculture was sunk to the lowest ebb.

These were the natural results of the inability of the General Government to regulate commerce, so as to prevent the injurious monopolies and exclusions of foreign nations, and the conflicting, and often ruinous regulations of the different States."

After the Constitution was drafted and ratified by the states, James Madison, among others, continued to be concerned about what they felt were many deficiencies in the Articles of Confederation, including having a damaging impact on commerce. In 1787, he wrote an appraisal of the Articles, listing their many defects. He discussed how the states' trade wars under the heading "Trespasses of the States on the rights of each other." States with prime port locations levied heavy taxes on adjoining states for their merchants to transport goods to other locations, an activity necessary for developing sustainable economic activity imperative for a state to grow and thrive.

 Madison wrote that "The practice of many States in restricting the commercial intercourse with other States, and putting their productions and manufactures on the same footing with those of foreign nations, though not contrary to the federal articles, is certainly adverse to the spirit of the Union, and tends to beget retaliating regulations, not less expensive & vexatious in themselves, than they are destructive of the general harmony."

Critics of the Articles of Confederation and of the arguments supportive of the Constitution commonly claim that the Framers wanted to promote commerce; however, the Commerce Clause was the specific solution to a specific problem, which was the initiation of trade barriers that threatened commerce and trade. "The Framers did not say that the Articles of Confederation were deficient because Congress lacked the power to set wages for workers or limit how much wheat a farmer could grow. If anyone suggested such a thing in Philadelphia, he might have been tarred and feathered." The

Framers clearly did not empower the federal government, explicitly or implied, to control the economy for any reason.

The Supreme Court's first encounter with the Commerce Clause occurred in 1824 in the case of Gibbons v. Ogden, in which it determined "Comprehensive as the word 'among' is, it may very properly be restricted to that commerce which concerns more States than one. . . . The genius and character of the whole government seem to be, that its action is to be applied to all the external concerns of the nation, and to those internal concerns which affect the States generally; but not to those which are completely within a particular State, which do not affect other States, and with which it is not necessary to interfere, for the purpose of executing some of the general powers of the government. The completely internal commerce of a State, then, may be considered as reserved for the State itself." The Court continued to uphold the Framers' intent for much of America's history, until a ruling in 1937, Jones v. Laughlin Steel Corp., where it decided that intrastate commercial activity does "have a close and substantial relation to interstate commerce [such] that their control is essential or appropriate to protect that commerce from burdens and obstruction."

The Supreme Court acknowledged the limits the Commerce Clause placed on Congress and the president during the early days of the New Deal. One of its more well-known decisions during that period of American history was the Court's striking down sections of the National Industrial Recovery Act of 1933 in the Schechter Poultry or "sick chicken" case, when it held that the Commerce Clause did not empower Congress to legislate setting wages and hours of poultry workers in Brooklyn, New York. The Court also found that the chickens never left New York, and explained "So far as the poultry here in question is concerned, the flow in interstate commerce had ceased. The poultry had come to permanent rest within the state. It was held, used or sold by defendants in relation to any further transaction in interstate commerce and was not destined for transportation to other states." The Court added "If the commerce clause were construed to reach all enterprises and transactions which could be said to have an indirect effect upon interstate commerce, the federal authority would embrace practically all the activities of the people."

In 1936, the Court ruled that another New Deal law, the Bituminous Coal Conservation Act, was unconstitutional. The Bituminous Coal Conservation Act created a national coal commission, with coal districts, and it fixed the prices of coal, as well as the wages, hours, and the working conditions of coal miners on a national basis. The Court concluded: "Much stress is put upon the evils which come from the struggle between employers and employees over the matter of wages, working conditions, the right of collective bargaining, etc., and the resulting strikes, curtailment and irregularity of production and effects on prices; and it is insisted that interstate commerce is greatly affected thereby. But, in addition to what has just been said, the conclusive answer is that the evils are all local evils over which the federal government has no legislative control."
President Franklin Roosevelt had had enough, and he threatened to replace current members of the Supreme Court with members who shared his ideas.

While the Court did begin to change its decisional foundation, Roosevelt did follow through with his threat and replaced retiring justices with lawyers who shared his contempt for the constitution's separation-of-powers. The Court soon began reversing prior decisions, starting with the 1937 decision in Jones v. Laughlin Steel Corp., opening the door for a major shift from the Constitution's Commerce Clause and the Framers' intent.

The most infamous of the Court's New Deal decisions was the 1942 ruling in Wickard v. Filburn. The Court turned from honoring the Constitution and the Framers' clear intentions, setting the stage for an outpouring of federal interventions in private economic activity. Removing any doubt of the direction the Court was headed, ruled that "noncommercial, local activity could be regulated by the federal government if it was said to have a substantial effect on commerce, even when it did not. Consequently, virtually any economic activity could be said to affect interstate commerce."

Since the Supreme Court under Roosevelt opened the flood gates, Congress has passed laws and federal departments and agencies have issued regulations affecting every aspect of economic activity. Rather than promoting commerce and trade by removing barriers between and among the states, "the indisputable rationale for the Commerce Clause, the federal government now intervenes in private economic activity, and stomps on state sovereignty, at every turn."

The Court has consistently determined that any federal law could affect commerce and would be constitutionally sustained, if Congress could provide a "rational basis" for law's impact on interstate commerce. Most laws are based on some type of rational basis. If they weren't, they would be irrational.

A notable decision in which the Court actually reverted back to the Framers' intent was written in 2000 in United States v. Morrison, which involved the Violence Against Women Act of 1994. The act created a federal cause of action for victims of gender-based violence, attempting to hand the federal government policing power that belonged to the states and its local governments. The Court found the attempt to create a link between the statute and interstate commerce was too vague. Supreme Court Justice William Rehnquist wrote, "We accordingly reject that argument that Congress may regulate noneconomic, violent criminal conduct based solely on that conduct's aggregate effect on interstate commerce. The Constitution requires a distinction between what is truly national and what is truly local."

Congress did not slow down, however, in its quest to gain more power and control over all economic activity and the states. As was predicted in the dissenting opinion in United States v. Morrison the federal government would soon attempt to regulate family matters. It has done just that, with its most notorious endeavor to date, Obamacare, with four justices concurring. Associate Justice Ruth Bader Ginsburg wrote, "[T]he decision to forgo insurance is hardly inconsequential or equivalent to 'doing nothing,'…it is, instead, an economic decision Congress has the authority to address under the Commerce Clause."

The federal government is perilously close to legislating every aspect of the lives of the American people. "Lest we forget, the

Supreme Court is ruling on laws passed by Congress and regulations issued by the executive branch." The proposed amendment returns the regulating commerce and trade to the parameters in the Constitution, encouraging commerce and trade between and among the states according to the Framers' intentions. As Dr. Milton Friedman explained: "Freedom in economic arrangements is itself a component of freedom broadly understood, so economic freedom is an end in itself. . . . [E]conomic freedom is also an indispensable means toward the achievement of political freedom."

AN AMENDMENT TO PROTECT PRIVATE PROPERTY

A core tenet of the Constitution lies in the essential foundation that ownership of private property is paramount to a successful society, and that safeguards must exist to protect against unrestrained government infringement. This principle was expressed by George Mason shortly before the drafting of the Declaration of Independence, who stated "…all men are created by nature equally free and independent and have certain inalienable rights…namely the enjoyment of life and liberty, with the means of acquiring and possessing property…"

The Framers understood that the right to own property was essential to a free and well-functioning society. They are more clear-cut on this principle than on any other. They relied heavily on John Locke's comments, and others, in stipulating the gravity of this essential doctrine. Locke's The Second Treatise of Government asserts, "[The government] cannot take from any man any part of his property without his consent. For the preservation of property being the end of government, and that for which men enter into society it necessarily supposes and requires, that the people should have property, without which they must be suppos'd to lose that by entering into society, which was the end for which they entered into it, too gross an absurdity for any man to own."

Also of profound influence was William Blackstone's Commentaries on the Laws of England, where he also acclaimed the virtues of the right to private property, stating "So great…is the regard for the law of private property, that it will not authorize the least violation of it; no, not even for the general good of the whole community.

If a new road, for instance, were to be made through the grounds of a private person, it might perhaps be extensively beneficial to the public; but the law permits no man, or set of men, to do this without the consent of the owner of the land." Blackstone further declared that the public good itself prioritized the protection of "every individual's private right, as modeled by the municipal law."

Property ownership is "the fruits of an individual's physical and intellectual labor" and is, without question, an inalienable right.

In the past, courts conservatively interpreted the Fifth Amendment, limiting government property seizure, or taking, to certain circumstances, such as for new highways, government offices, and military bases. The straightforward provisions in the Constitution for the protection of rights and adequate compensation in the event of infringement by regulation as well as a taking of part or all of the property, was honorably adhered to for the first half of our nation's post-Constitution history.

Now, the courts allow the government to seize property to "increase the general public welfare," such as when the government uses the doctrine of eminent domain to take private property to facilitate a private development that will raise the government's tax revenues. The unquestionable provisions of the Constitution have been intentionally muddied. The 1978 decision in Penn Central Transp. V. New York City, for instance, proclaimed there is no "set formula" for determining what constitutes a taking as opposed to a partial taking, and therefore, determining a remedy is nearly impossible. What was clearly set forth in the Constitution has been twisted to produce ambiguity that severely diminishes the rights of the individual and dramatically inflates the government's power to do as they wish with no consequences.

The proposed amendment acknowledges the original intent and provisions set forth by the Framers in the Constitution, and once again clarifies what is and is not acceptable government action. In addition, the proposed amendment clarifies the parameters of loss of property rights through regulation, partial taking, and a complete taking, as well as specifies circumstances for applying a remedy.

AN AMENDMENT TO GRANT THE STATES AUTHORITY TO DIRECTLY AMEND THE CONSTITUTION

Remember that Article V of the Constitution enumerates the processes for amending the Constitution. As the text and history shows, the processes are difficult and time-consuming. This is intentional, for the Framers were confident that they set forth a document that would withstand the tests of time and circumstance, and the ability to easily change it would break down the provisions and protections carefully built into it.
In spite the care put into composing the Constitution, the post-constitutional period, particularly the past 75 years, has deconstructed much of it.

Our federal government has evolved into the very animal the Framers warned about and the Constitution protected against. Rather than abide by it, the three branches of government, particularly the executive branch, has blatantly ignored it, enacting regulations and laws that essentially rewrite it and render many parts of it obsolete, to the detriment of this country. "The Statists have constructed an all-powerful centralized federal government, unleashing endless social experiments in pursuit of utopian designs. The federal branches have used judicial review, congressional delegation, broad abuses of the Commerce and Takings clauses, and the power of the purse (taxing, spending, and borrowing), among other things, to commandeer the sovereignty of the states and citizenry."

Woodrow Wilson openly discredited the principles so carefully engrained into the Constitution, openly declaring "No doubt a great deal of nonsense has been talked about the inalienable rights of the individual, and a great deal that was mere vague sentiment and pleasing speculation has been put forth as fundamental principle...the individual is without independent. God-given natural rights which form the basis for America's founding. The Constitution's text and the Framers' intent are of no consequence—

unless, of course, they can be said to justify if not compel the republic's self-mutilation."

Since Wilson's presidency, there have been several presidents who strived to move this country back to its original intended states; however, the decline has been faster than restoration. The author notes in Liberty and Tyranny, "So distant is America today from its founding principles that it is difficult to precisely describe the nature of American government. It is not strictly a constitutional republic, because the Constitution has been and continues to be easily altered by a judicial oligarchy that mostly enforces, if not expands, the Statist's agenda. It is not strictly a representative republic, because so many edicts are produced by a maze of administrative departments that are unknown to the public and detached from its sentiment. It is not strictly a federal republic, because the states that gave the central government life now live at its behest. What, then, is it? It is a society steadily transitioning toward statism..."

The proposed amendment would allow states to bypass Congress altogether, empowering them to check Congress and more fully represent the will of the American people. There is no persuasive justification for states to be forced to go through Congress to amend the Constitution, when Congress itself will, and has, barred efforts to correct the flagrant abuse of power by the federal government. The states would be able to amend the Constitution themselves, with a two-thirds consensus, and without a convention. The proposed amendment also places a six-year time limit on the time that a proposal is introduced, considered, and adopted. In addition, the proposed amendment may not be altered during that six-year time period, and once an amendment is ratified, the decision cannot be reversed.

AN AMENDMENT TO GRANT THE STATES AUTHORITY TO CHECK CONGRESS

Just as the amendment process is difficult, the process for pushing a bill through Congress is just as cumbersome and sometimes impossible. Just as the Framers intended the amendment process to be relatively difficult to prevent hasty change, they also built a degree of difficulty into the process of making and changing laws for the same reason.

However, the modern Congress has compounded the methodology in efforts to make it impossible to oppose or correct their exploits. As a result, a few key and heavily-influential leaders in Congress, as well as the president himself, repeatedly evades committee and subcommittee hearings, public comment and the entire legislative process, concealing significant details of sizeable legislation or stopgap measures from members of Congress and attentive US citizens. This arbitrary exercise of power not afforded them has sinister implications for the preservation of America as a free nation.

Thomas Jefferson cautioned against these very practices, and addressed this very weakness in a letter to James Madison dated December 20, 1787. The Constitution had just been adopted and was waiting ratification by the states. Jefferson note the evil of legislating in this manner, writing "The instability of our laws is really an immense evil. I think it would be well to provide in our constitutions that there shall always be a twelvemonth between ingrossing [form of "engrossing" that is no longer used, which in this case means to provide the final written copy or manuscript] a bill and passing it; that it should then be offered to its passage without changing a word; and that if circumstances should be thought to require a speedier passage, it should take two thirds of both houses instead of a bare majority."

The passage of Obamacare, a law nearly 3,000 pages long, is the most recent example of the necessity of these safeguards. Obamacare barely passed with a 219-212, with no Republican votes, and no final version even being available for review. The 219 members of Congress who voted to pass did not even know all of the provisions of the bill. Nancy Pelosi, Speaker of the House at the time, declared to the Legislative Conference for the National Association of Counties, "We have to pass the bill so that you can find out what is in it..." Some members of Congress do not even bother to hide the fact they habitually circumvent the legislative process. Voting members of Congress did not have all of the facts about Obamacare, and the public had even less.

Since it passed three years ago, the American public still does not know everything Obamacare mandates. Regardless, thousands of additional pages of regulations have been issued by the Department of Health and Human Services, the Internal Revenue Service and other federal administration organizations, and the extent of the controls, mandates and financial burden has still not been fully revealed. Many of these regulations and compliance controls are in direct violation of the Constitution and existing federal statute. Recently, Congress passed the Violence Against Women Reauthorization Act of 2013 (VAWA). Congress is very good at naming bills with misleading and emotional hooks that makes it difficult to publicly oppose them. The VAWA is a good example. This bill was signed into law with no meaningful debate, and with no opportunity for amendment.

"Despite its title, the law is deeply flawed, as numerous commentators have noted, and raises serious doubts about its constitutionality in several respects, including the fundamental right to free speech and due process." The act also redefines domestic violence to include "emotional distress" or the use of "unpleasant speech," descriptors that are so subjective and vague that it throws the door wide open for the government to trample an individual's rights for just about anything, voiding the original act of any semblance of being reasonable. In addition, the act grants visas to illegal aliens who claim to be victims of domestic abuse, which, according to the language of the most recent version of the act, could be defined as anything. The states have already address domestic violence effectively. This is not to say that a federal role, in certain circumstances, is illegitimate or unnecessary. United States v.

Morrison, the Supreme Court decided in 2000 that parts of the first VAWA were unconstitutional, holding that "…the act exceeded congressional authority under the Commerce Clause and Fourteenth Amendment."

"When Congress passes immense and complex bills that virtually no one can comprehend, and often without constitutional power, and further delegates independent authority to the executive branch in violation of the separation-of-powers doctrine to pile regulations on top of laws—resulting in thousands of additional pages of rules—is this not the "Despotism, or unlimited Sovereignty, or absolute Power . . . [of] a Majority of a popular Assembly" of which John Adams warned?" Opposition expressed about VAWA has nothing to do with protecting victims of violence, but argues against Congress's continued willingness to heavily violate the Constitution.

The proposed amendment would provide a means to simplify both processes when situations arise that need more immediate resolution. It prevents Congress from passing exceedingly large and unintelligible bills, often outside the legislative process, and delegating additional authority to the executive branch and administrative organizations who throw on countless regulations, further convoluting the issue about which the bill was first introduced. Such practices further distance law makers from citizens, make public scrutiny, transparency and accountability impossible. The proposed amendment would reinstate a Constitutional process for passing bills through Congress, and would remove barriers to citizen participation.

AN AMENDMENT TO PROTECT THE VOTE

The proposed amendment is to protect the American people's vote. It requires voters to present some form of government-issued picture identification that was obtained in manner that verified citizenship, and provides that the federal government provide free identification for those who would otherwise be unable to obtain identification because they cannot afford associated fees.

The typical counterargument whenever voter fraud is mentioned is "There is no voter fraud," that there are only occasional and isolated incidents that occur. However, research conducted by election experts John Fund and Hans von Spakovsky revealed that the integrity of our voting system is largely compromised in two ways, one of which is voter registration and voting by non-US citizens documented in every state in the country, and intentional fraud. The refusal of the federal government to enforce the law makes both of them commonplace.

Fund and von Spakovsky demonstrated that illegal aliens are, in fact, registered and active voters in federal, state and local elections. The federal government even acknowledges it, stating "There is no reliable method of determining the number of non-citizens registered, or actually voting, because most laws meant to ensure that only citizens vote are ignored, are inadequate, or are systematically undermined by government officials. Those who ignore the implications of noncitizen voting are wilfully blind to the problem, or may actually approve of illegal voting."

The Government Accountability Office (GAO) found in 2005 that up to 3 percent of registered voters were not citizens of the U.S. Moreover, Scott Gessler, Colorado's secretary of state, testified before Congress in 2011 that more than 11,000 registered voters in Colorado may not be U.S. citizens, and almost half of them voted. The nonpartisan research organization, the Pew Center on the States, reported in 2012 that "there are more than 1.8 million deceased individuals who remain on the voter registration rolls. In addition, approximately 2.75 million people have registrations in more than one state. Moreover, as many as 24 million—one in every eight—voter registrations in the United States are no longer valid or are significantly inaccurate."

Pennsylvania and Arizona both took steps to mitigate these voter-related issues. The state of Pennsylvania enacted a law in 2012 that requires a state-issued photo ID to vote.

Those who could not afford the fees would be issued a free ID. Opposition argued that the law as racist and an attempt to suppress minority voting. The American Civil Liberties Union (ACLU) and the National Association for the Advancement of Colored People (NAACP) filed suit, arguing that the law was designed to prevent between 100,000 and 500,000 people from voting; however, they were unable to produce a single person who would be prevented from voting under the new law. The bill was signed into law by the Governor, but was delayed from taking effect until after the 2012 election by the Pennsylvania Supreme Court, who cited that "administrative issues was the basis for the delay."

Arizona amended the state's voter registration process in 2004 by requiring proof of citizenship at the time of voter registration. This provision became law in 2005 and prevention 20,000 ineligible individuals from registering to vote; however, several civil rights organizations filed a law suit, claiming that the law unfairly targeted Native Americans, Hispanics and other minority groups by enacting a poll tax. The Ninth Circuit Court of Appeals eventually ruled that the law did not enact a poll tax, but was superseded by a federal law that establishes voter registration requirements. The U.S. Supreme Court ruled in June of 2013 that a state cannot require proof of citizenship when an individual is filing a federal voter registration form, but can do so if they are filing a state voter registration form, which those intending to break the law are highly unlikely to do.

Contrary to the ruling in the Arizona case, Article I, Section 2, Clause I of the Constitution, the Elector Qualifications Clause, provides, "…the Electors in each State shall have the Qualifications requisite for Electors of the most numerous Branch of the State Legislature." The clause states plainly that Congress shall regulate the time, place and manner for holding elections, and has nothing to do with setting voter registration requirements. Approximately 15 states to date are considering voting reform, including voter registration requirements.

The Civil Rights Act of 1964 and the Voting Rights Act of 1965 were implemented as temporary measure to enforce the Thirteenth, Fourteenth and Fifteenth post-Civil War Amendment, preventing discrimination in voting procedures, which included banning poll taxes, literary tests and any other measures enacted intentionally to prevent certain groups from voting, and allowing an individual to sue should they be discriminated against. These temporary acts have been repeatedly extended and broadened, most recently in 2006, when it was extended another 25 years. While the Supreme Court ruled in June of 2013 that it was no longer justifiable to continue to authorize these two acts, it preserved the right to sue if discriminated against. In addition, two other laws overseeing state voting processes, the National Voter Registration Act of 1993 and the Help America Vote Act of 2002, both impose restrictions on states to regulate elections, leaving the door wide open for continued fraud.

The proposed amendment also revises early voting, voting by mail, and ensures security for electronic voting procedures. Currently, early voting can take place so early, that conditions can change dramatically, and those voting on Election Day may be voting with a completely different set of information than early voters. Limiting early voting to a few weeks before Election Day, except in the case of military members, would virtually eliminate this disparity. Furthermore, it removes the potential for fraud in circumstances in which an individual does not vote in person, either by mail or via electronic vote, and requires verified effective security measures to be in place to avoid tampering, hacking, data manipulation or cyber attacks.

EPILOGUE THE TIME FOR ACTION

There is little doubt that, should they be confronted directly with their blatant usurping of our Constitution and its provisions, as well as protections, the offending members of our federal government will continue to assault our foundational principles. Their ongoing efforts to increase their own ambitious power and to decrease potential opposition will continue unassuaged, with any and all efforts to check their tyrannical pursuits countered by fierce cries of heretical interference. Significant and consistent action by the American people is paramount to our getting this country back on track. It will not be easy, nor will it be a quick turnaround. Years of misbehavior got us to this point, and it will take years to correct; however, we are at a pivotal point in our nation's history, and time is running short. Soon, it will simply be too late—we must act now.

We have lost sight of what our Constitution laid as a foundation for our country's governance. We must return to our Constitutional roots, initiated by the study of our history and a fond familiarity with this sacred document. Those who oppose various provisions of our Constitution are not, however, without value to this process, for their opinions merit honest evaluation of our country's condition and the potential need for addressing problems. Responding with an equally narrow sighted vision and tyrannical outlook on the opposite end of the current spectrum will only serve to perpetuate that which needs to be checked and balanced. All debate and evidence is important, and must be considered equally to fully embrace, once again, the American dream. The American people must be free again to determine their own fate.

As President Ronald Reagan once said, "You and I have a rendezvous with destiny. We will preserve for our children this, the last best hope of man on earth, or we will sentence them to take the first step into a thousand years of darkness. If we fail, at least our children and our children's children say of us that we justified our brief moment here. We did all that can be done." We have not yet done all that can be done.

CPSIA information can be obtained at www.ICGtesting.com
Printed in the USA
BVOW07s0203091013

333262BV00007B/92/P